T0146844

THE PRACTICAL STRATEGIES SERIES
IN GIFTED EDUCATION

series editors
FRANCES A. KARNES & KRISTEN R. STEPHENS

Advocacy for Gifted Children and Gifted Programs

Joan D. Lewis, Ph.D.

Routledge
Taylor & Francis Group

NEW YORK AND LONDON

First published 2008 by Prufrock Press Inc.

Published 2021 by Routledge
605 Third Avenue, New York, NY 10017
2 Park Square, Milton Park, Abingdon, Oxon OX14 4RN

Routledge is an imprint of the Taylor & Francis Group, an informa business

ISBN 13: 978-1-59363-318-9 (pbk)

Contents

The Practical Strategies Series in Gifted Education offers teachers, counselors, administrators, parents, and other interested parties up-to-date instructional techniques and information on a variety of issues pertinent to the field of gifted education. Each guide addresses a focused topic and is written by scholars with authority on the issue. Several guides have been published. Among the titles are:

- *Acceleration Strategies for Teaching Gifted Learners*
- *Curriculum Compacting: An Easy Start to Differentiating for High-Potential Students*
- *Enrichment Opportunities for Gifted Learners*
- *Independent Study for Gifted Learners*
- *Motivating Gifted Students*
- *Questioning Strategies for Teaching the Gifted*
- *Social & Emotional Teaching Strategies*
- *Using Media & Technology With Gifted Learners*

For a current listing of available guides within the series, please contact Prufrock Press at (800) 998-2208 or visit http://www.prufrock.com.

Supporters of gifted education for their own children, as well as all gifted learners, need to develop the skills of advocacy in order to build strong, lasting programs. Appropriate education for gifted learners has not been a priority of the education community. If no one speaks up on behalf of these learners, who will? This volume describes a wide variety of strategies that can be used to advocate for gifted students at different levels.

"Gifted education is not about status, it is about meeting student needs" (National Association for Gifted Children [NAGC], n.d., ¶6). Myths about gifted children flourish, often limiting their educational opportunities. Well-informed and energetic advocates are needed to change local and national perceptions in this area of education. Gifted children are not more important than other students, nor are they less important. All children deserve to learn at a level suited to their abilities every day in school, rather than waste time doing irrelevant and inappropriate work. In addition, children deserve teachers who are prepared and knowledgeable about their educational needs. Making these worthy goals a reality for gifted learners will require supporters to build their understanding about effective tools for advocacy.

Advocacy for the Gifted

Gifted learners need the efforts of strong supporters who will advocate for their educational needs. This volume applies the five "W's" and an "H" strategy to advocacy for gifted education: Who, What, When, Where, Why, and How. Several authors, among them, James Gallagher (1997), speak to the need of *all* children to receive an education that is appropriate for their educational abilities. Gallagher emphasizes that gifted students are an underserved population. In order for this neglect to be reversed in public and private schools, supporters need to learn how to be effective advocates. It is not enough to discuss the characteristics and learning needs of gifted children among fellow supporters; the message must be conveyed to broader audiences of prospective converts (Karnes & Lewis, 1997).

Advocacy in support of appropriate educational opportunities for gifted learners is a necessity. There is no federal mandate; individual states provide varying levels of service. Some states identify gifted learners as early as kindergarten, whereas others don't require identification. States offer various options, which include individual education plans of one kind or another, services for different levels of giftedness, part-time homeschooling, programs for twice-exceptional students, acceleration, and early college/dual enrollment (Hoagies' Gifted Education Page, n.d.). Although more states are providing a wider range of options for gifted learners than in the past, service is still inconsistent, frequently permissive rather than required, and not comprehensive for all ages. In addition, in the absence of a federal mandate, state mandates can be withdrawn at any time with no penalty.

Why does there continue to be so little support for gifted education when the function of schools is to teach all children? Undoubtedly, many causes contribute to this inequity. One reason is very few teacher education programs require a class that provides more than a brief mention of the characteristics and resulting educational and affective needs of gifted learners. Consequently, teachers often are unaware that some children are capable of learning at a vastly more advanced level than other children in their grade. Differences in learning ability are difficult to see unless instructional opportunities allow open-ended demonstrations of knowledge and skills.

Some gifted learners "advertise themselves" with their probing questions and depth of knowledge. They may be seeking attention for their wide range of advanced skills, or they may not be able to disguise their abilities due to their intense enthusiasm for learning. Sometimes this obvious display of advanced abilities is recognized by teachers and appropriate educational options are offered. However, some teachers may be annoyed or intimidated by these students' intensities and neglect their educational needs altogether.

Peer relations often are another source of stress for gifted children because they tend to have more advanced friendship needs (Gross, 2002). Such students develop a variety of responses to the growing realization that they aren't like others their age. Peers may tease or bully bright youth because they are different. As a result, already strained social interactions with peers can deteriorate.

Some students become more assertive in demonstrating their skills, and others may pursue their own interests quietly.

A sizable number of children with gifted abilities strive to hide among the crowd by intentionally or unintentionally under-achieving. Although a few gifted individuals need individual or group counseling, all gifted learners need guidance to help them learn to understand themselves and make the most of their abilities. They also need academic and career counseling con-siderably earlier than other students because of their advanced intellectual abilities and often more intense emotional responses (Silverman, 1993).

Counselors, like teachers, rarely receive specialized training in preparation for working with gifted students in schools and communities. Why this dearth of preparation of educators and counselors? First, gifted individuals make up a small percentage of the general population, the number ranging from 1% or 2% to as high as 15% or even 20% depending on the definition of giftedness. The vast majority of students in any classroom fall into the "average" category, and it is this group on which teach-ers tend to focus. Those students whose abilities fall outside this middle range are not as well served. Although some teachers do an excellent job of teaching children in a way that suits their indi-vidual needs, not enough teachers recognize the many differences between children and how these variations impact learning.

In the United States, society has struggled with intellectual differences between citizens. Equality of all citizens is a cor-nerstone of this nation, yet, whether we like it or not, some people are more advanced and skilled in various ways than oth-ers. Generally speaking, our society is more accepting of dif-ferences in ability that are not intellectual or academic. Clark (2008) points out the paradox that results from wanting high achievement at home and abroad but resenting when one person is noticeably more capable than another.

These two beliefs—a distrust of the intellect and an assumption that people should be allowed to develop to their full potential—have clashed throughout American history and have muddled effort to provide a quality education for the nation's most promising students. (O'Connell-Ross, 1993, p. 13)

Providing a challenging curriculum for gifted learners risks running afoul of educators and community members who cry "elitism" because the instruction differs in content or pace from the general curriculum. Branding gifted education as elitist has provided an excuse not to offer programs for gifted students (Clark, 2008). Varsity athletics provide specialized opportunities for students who have advanced physical skills, but they are not considered elitist. Instead, they are frequently and strongly supported by the school district and community (Gallagher & Gallagher, 1994). Is the problem "a distrust of the intellect" as O'Connell-Ross (1993, p. 13) wrote? Likewise, popular magazine articles written for parents display titles such as "Is Your Child Learning Too Fast?" and "Help, My Child Is Gifted!" (Lewis & Karnes, 1996).

In order to advocate successfully, supporters must do their homework. First, advocates need to inform themselves about the characteristics and educational needs of gifted learners. One way to accomplish this basic task is to take a college class about gifted education. However, as informative as this method is, it is not always practical. A simpler approach is to read one or more of the many books and journal articles that have been written about gifted children. Professional journal articles are recommended over articles published in popular magazines because they usually are written by specialists in the field rather than staff writers. Web pages are another ready source of information on any topic; however, they must be selected carefully because no special review of their content is required for publication. A selection of books, professional articles, and reliable Web sources is provided in the Resources section.

The next step in effective advocacy will require some detective work in order to uncover past and present issues surrounding gifted education, first locally and then statewide and nationally. The aim is to develop an understanding of the context for advocacy. A good place to begin is to attend and join a parent support group for gifted education and talk with members. Seek out the officers and ask about the local gifted education regulations and policies. Other local sources of information are teachers of the gifted and the district administrator who is responsible for the program. The state director for gifted education is a valuable source for local, state, and national information and current legislation pertaining to gifted education. Use state gifted organization and national association Web sites to gain further insight about gifted children, current issues, and legislative updates.

Armed with facts about the characteristics of gifted children and their resulting educational needs, as well as local, state, and national perspectives, advocates are prepared to make meaningful contributions to public relations and advocacy efforts.

Lewis and Karnes (2005) contended that advocacy differs from public relations and lobbying, although some of the strategies are similar. They defined advocacy as "the act or process of advocating or supporting a cause or proposal" (p. 616), such as preparing written campaign materials for a favorite running for public office or speaking on behalf of a candidate, whereas public relations in education consists of "a systematically and continuously planned, executed, and evaluated program of interactive communication and human relations" (as cited in Kowalski, 1996, p. 7). Lobbying, often confused with advocacy, describes

> activities aimed at influencing public officials and especially members of a legislative body on legislation. 1) to promote (as a project) or secure the passage of legislation by influencing public officials. 2) to attempt to influence or sway (as a public official) toward a desired action. (Lewis & Karnes, 2005, p. 616)

Advocacy, then, is actively and voluntarily supporting a particular cause, such as the value of and need for gifted education. Much of the earlier literature written in support of gifted education was aimed at educating the public about gifted children and gifted programs. The strategies that were used can be employed to build support for meeting the needs of gifted learners. Personal characteristics that aid one in becoming a successful advocate are energy, enthusiasm, objective and logical thinking, ability to anticipate opposition, persistence, and a willingness to express appreciation for even small gains toward a large end.

Why Advocate?

Few members of the general public and a surprisingly small number of educators have a genuine awareness about gifted learners and the kinds of education they require both cognitively and affectively. General education teachers, school counselors, principals, and other administrators receive little or no instruction regarding the education of gifted students (Besnoy, 2005). Furthermore, myths and misunderstandings reinforce stereotyping and lead to inappropriate instruction (Clark, 2008). Roeper (1986) reported that gifted students have "become the educationally disadvantaged children in America" (p. 6). Gifted programs may be among the first to lose funding when budgets are tight (Kiger, 1998), perhaps because they are believed to be elitist (Clark, 2008; Karnes, Lewis, & Stephens, 1999). "Opponents are vocal; supporters need to speak out, too" (Karnes et al., 1999, p. 15).

In the past, newspapers have printed little about gifted students and their unique education unless there was a perceived problem or inequity—then, articles highlighting discrepancies tended to be printed over a short period of time (Karnes & Lewis, 1995; Meadows & Karnes, 1992). Magazine articles also are few and infrequent (Lewis & Karnes, 1996). Communicating accurate information is crucial (Karnes & Lewis, 1997; Karnes et al., 1999; Lewis & Karnes, 2005), first to provide knowledge to educators so they recognize that what is developmentally appropriate for the majority of students usually is not sufficiently challenging or fast paced enough for gifted learners in their areas of strength (Clark, 2008). In addition, individuals who control the disbursement of educational funds and those who vote on school bonds need to be well informed about the educational and affective needs of this population so they receive the counseling, career, and academic guidance needed to make full use of their intellectual, academic, creative, artistic, and leadership abilities. The second reason for distributing accurate information is to correct misinformation that may prevail, such as "gifted children can learn on their own without teacher assistance" or "they will benefit from being classroom tutors." One of the biggest myths in education is that everyone must be taught the same thing in the same way at the same time to be equitable (Clark, 2008). This method would be similar to making the arbitrary pronouncement that because many people need to wear glasses in order to see, everyone must not only need glasses but also must use the same prescription. One-size-fits-all education is no more equitable than telling children who are deaf or hard of hearing that they must leave their hearing aids at home because it is not fair to the rest of the students for these children to receive special treatment.

Many myths and misunderstandings need to be corrected and replaced with accurate information through advocacy efforts. Listed below are common gifted education myths that can limit education opportunities for gifted students.

1. Gifted students don't need help; they'll do fine on their own.
2. Teachers challenge all the students, so gifted kids will be fine in the regular classroom.
3. Gifted students make everyone else in the class smarter by providing a role model or a challenge.

4. All children are gifted.
5. Acceleration options, such as early entrance, grade skipping, or early exit, can be socially harmful for gifted students.
6. Gifted education programs are elitist.
7. A student can't be gifted if he or she is making poor grades.
8. Gifted students are happy, popular, and well adjusted in school.
9. A student can't be gifted if he or she has a learning disability or qualifies for other special education services. (NAGC, n.d.)

Clark (2008) also discusses common erroneous beliefs about gifted children. Her first two examples appear on the previous list, and her remaining examples enlarge and extend the critical issues identified by NAGC. The following are quoted from Clark's well-respected text *Growing Up Gifted* (2008):

1. *All children are gifted.* All children are valuable, all children are important, and all children should be allowed to develop to their highest potential; however, all children are not gifted. . . .
2. *Gifted students are not at risk. If they were really gifted, they can get by on their own.* . . . The well-documented fact is that intelligence is developed from an interaction between genetic patterns and environmental opportunities. It is dynamic rather than fixed, which puts children who are not stimulated at the level of their growth at risk. They do not progress; rather, they regress. . . .
3. *Giftedness can easily be measured by intelligence tests and tests of achievement.* . . . Although current intelligence tests give valuable estimates of abilities in the area of intelligence that can be predictive of success on school-related tests, these tests cannot identify giftedness in many areas of intelligence or suggest an individual's potential. Identification of giftedness is a complex task and requires a variety of samples of a person's abilities from many areas of function.

4. *A good teacher can teach any student because good teaching is all that is needed. What is good for gifted students is good for everyone.* Although good teaching practices must be the basis for all teaching excellence, the appropriate education of gifted students does not end with these important concepts and strategies . . . teachers of the gifted and talented need some special skills. . . .

5. *If you accelerate the curriculum for all students, you do not need programs for gifted learners.* . . . One of the commonly accepted characteristics found as the brain becomes more efficient and expresses higher levels of intelligence is the increased speed of thought processing. Gifted students learn faster and process information more quickly. . . .

6. *You really learn something when you teach it. It never hurts students to review what they have learned.* This belief has led to the practice of using gifted students as tutors for slower students in the classroom and having them do more work at the same level. Such activities have been used to fill the time of the student who finishes assigned work quickly, relieving the teacher of additional planning for such a student and simultaneously providing help to students who require extra support. . . . (pp. 21–23)

Who will advocate for gifted learners? Every individual concerned about the education of gifted learners can become an advocate. Otherwise, gifted learners in this country will continue to be underserved. These students lose the guidance they need to stretch their abilities to the fullest just when they are discovering their learning passions. The community and the larger world lose the full talents of promising citizens. To quote the United Negro College Fund, "A mind is a terrible thing to waste" (as cited in Roberts & Inman, 2003).

Who Can Advocate?

Teachers and coordinators of gifted learners; parents, guardians, and caregivers; the students themselves; and others in the community all have strengths to bring to the important task of advocacy for the gifted.

Teachers and Coordinators of the Gifted

These individuals bring their knowledge and day-to-day experience with gifted students to the table. Although they are restricted in some advocacy opportunities because they are employed by the educational system, many avenues are open for them to make a difference in the life of a child. They can:

- Share what they have learned about students' educational and affective needs in a friendly manner in their formal and informal conversations with other educators. Getting information out regarding best practices will have a cumulative impact over time. Teachers tend to talk about what works or does not work. Adding one's voice to this conversation about the needs of gifted students is a powerful form of advocacy. Besnoy (2005) suggested collaborating with colleagues in demonstrating effective instructional strategies for working with gifted learners.

- Network with other school employees such as the counselor, library media specialist, special subject teachers (e.g., art, music, P.E.), and nonteaching staff. These individuals provide subject-specific instruction and support for gifted children in important areas of learning. The secretary and custodian often play the vital roles of friend and confidant for many children. They all need to have an understanding of gifted children in order to work with them effectively.

- Build relationships with the principal and other administrators. Such a practice is vital to the health of a school and district gifted program. Lewis, Cruzeiro, and Hall (2007) found that gifted education may not be considered part of the school improvement plan. As some of the best-informed members of the district when it comes to gifted education, teachers and coordinators of the gifted are well-positioned to insist that gifted education goals be included in data collection and analysis. They can make certain that there are goals with regard to the gifted program to be evaluated. Besnoy (2005) suggested inviting administrators to observe or participate in a concluding activity in the gifted classroom. They can witness first-hand the capabilities of these advanced learners. Special events like these make excellent photo opportunities that can be published in the local paper, district or school newsletter, and on Web sites.

- Ask local, state, and even national governmental leaders to make a guest appearance in the gifted classroom. They might be asked to judge the finished products of a major activity or observe an academic or fine arts performance. Law makers who have a history of voting for gifted education can be awarded framed certificates of thanks for their support. Pictures of this kind of event are usually well-received by newspapers. Again, the photo could be prominently placed on the school Web site and in other school or district publications.

- Invite members of the professional community, business leaders, and others from the local and surrounding communities to the gifted classroom for various events. Karnes and Stephens (2000) suggested asking professionals in a particular field to evaluate the quality of student products, such as having an architect judge student house plans. The students benefit from receiving feedback from a specialist in the field and the professional is impressed by what is going on in the gifted classroom. These are examples of public relations strategies that help others develop an understanding of gifted education by building relationships with the students themselves.

- Work within the system to encourage ongoing staff development on cognitive and affective characteristics, identification, differentiation, acceleration, counseling, and articulated programs for Pre-K–12. Karnes and Lewis (1996) suggested using a variety of videotapes about gifted students and classroom instruction in staff development when experts are not available. Building a library of authoritative videotapes or DVDs for the district or even sharing between districts can bring some of the experts in the field of gifted education into staff development sessions.

- Teach gifted students skills in public relations. Bisland (2003) described what students gain from developing the critical process skills used for public relations such as problem solving, written communication, and oral communication. Students can brainstorm the features of their program to share with the school or community. Through simulations, students can practice planning a public relations event; developing materials such as brochures, a cover letter to include in a mailing, and a news release about the event; and practice being interviewed on a television or radio news program (Bisland, 2003).

- Support an existing parent group or organize a group if there is none. Neighboring districts or the state gifted association can be contacted (see Web Resources) for support materials and speakers to help build the organization. If a group is well established and effective, then reach out to new groups or volunteer with the state association.
- Identify parents and others who would make good advocates locally and statewide. They may only need a nudge to become involved and discover the power they have in persuading others to see the value in supporting gifted education.

Parents, Guardians, and Caregivers

Securing the future of gifted education depends on building partnerships between parents and teachers (Karnes et al., 1999). Parents, guardians, and other caregivers have a lot of untapped power. When channeled, this power can make important changes in the understanding of school personnel, community members, relatives, and legislators. Parents, guardians, and caregivers can advocate in the following ways:

- Advocate for the specific needs of their child by visiting with teachers, the principal, and the school counselor. They should remember to respect the needs of all children, yet be firm in communicating their child's individual needs.
- Form and work with a parent support group to make use of combined strengths—there is power in numbers. When everyone speaks from the same platform, a united parent group can be very effective in advocating for all gifted learners in the school district instead of just isolated, individual children. Gifted children have a better chance of being served effectively when all parties work together. Nevertheless, it takes that first voice speaking up on behalf of gifted learners for any help to be initiated. Parents, guardians, and caregivers can be that voice.

- Join together with a few other like-minded parents or guardians to talk to teachers, the principal, the school counselor, or members of the school board. Several parents/guardians together are more likely to command attention than just one alone.

Roberts and Inman (2003) provided a sizable list of advocacy activities specifically for parents, from partnering with teachers and schools, running for the school board, and joining and advocating with local, state, and national gifted organizations; to writing letters to the editor, making presentations to the school board, and developing a video about gifted children.

Gifted Students

Students need only a little direction to become valuable advocates for their own interests, as well as for the instruction being provided. Gifted students can be valuable spokespersons for their gifted program whether they realize it or not. When gifted students attend their gifted class, a special seminar, or other educational opportunity, they often enjoy the experience so much that they return to class describing what they did as "playing games," thus perpetuating the common misperception that they receive unfair extras that all students would enjoy. Gifted students need to learn to describe what they do in their gifted classes more accurately and without an air of superiority.

One method for dispelling this misinformation is to allow gifted students to invite a friend to visit the class every quarter. The invited students usually are excited about attending and look forward to the opportunity. The gifted students can plan the agenda, selecting those activities they especially enjoy and others that are satisfyingly challenging. A mix of fun and challenge gives the visitors a better picture of the gifted program. Choice of activities will depend on the age and interests of both the gifted students and their guests. Visitors will leave talking about what those "unfair extras" are really like.

With adult direction, gifted students can do the following:

- Learn how to advocate for their own educational opportunities in a positive way. Instruction in student advocacy should take into consideration the age of the children. Teachers and parents can teach students appropriate ways to ask teachers for more information about a subject the class is studying, nonthreatening methods for disagreeing with facts the teacher has presented, and how to suggest a different assignment for one that is too easy or repetitious. Some gifted children are used as classroom tutors when they finish assignments early. As a result, they need to learn how and when to ask for alternatives to tutoring so they can extend their own learning.

- Write letters to the school board and local and national government leaders, and make appointments to talk to these leaders about the benefits of gifted programs and services. They also can advocate through demonstration of their mastery of and their excitement for high-level learning opportunities at public meetings and events. For example, students can attend a school board meeting and submit their names to be on the agenda to speak to the board. Similarly, students can attend a state board of education meeting and speak for or against a particular cause.

- Tour the capitol as a group, preferably wearing T-shirts bearing their school and program names. Younger students might deliver thank-you notes and treats to the education or appropriations committee or for all the legislators. Older students can discuss the value of gifted education for them personally with legislators and staffers alike. In some instances, these older students might have the opportunity to testify to the benefits of gifted education at a subcommittee hearing when an important piece of legislation is pending.

- Share and display news articles describing their performances at various competitions on the classroom wall or bulletin board. Awards from these competitions might be profiled in school display cases along with athletic trophies.

- Utilize their technology skills to create graphics for teacher and school use and to search out quality Web sites pertinent to course content. They also can create Web pages for individual teachers. A much more challenging learning and advocacy opportunity would be to develop Web Quests for teachers to use with their classes on a variety of single subjects and interdisciplinary units. Web Quests could even be developed focusing on gifted education and targeted at parents, educators, business people, and the media.

Others in the Community

Other people in the community may be supportive of gifted education even if they do not have a gifted child, grandchild, or other relative. They can be invited to volunteer, join support groups, and use their unique skills to help advocate for the education of the gifted.

Advocacy and public relations can extend far beyond the local community. Becoming active in the state gifted association widens the reach of any one advocate and is not limited to education professionals; parents, guardians, and any interested community member are welcome. State-level associations also can join forces to broaden the public relations and advocacy efforts of each group; however, this strategy has not been adopted often (Riley & Karnes, 1993; Troxclair & Karnes, 1997).

How Can I Advocate?

Prior to beginning any advocacy efforts, there are several steps necessary that will increase one's ability to be a proactive advocate. Even when initiating only one or two small activities, it is important to have an organized plan. The recommendations that follow supply practical ideas that will save time and make all advocacy efforts more effective.

Involve Others

Seek out and include other people who can help spread the intended message. Lewis and Karnes (2005) described the multiple connections enjoyed with friends and acquaintances in different spheres, such as school, career, social, spiritual, community, and financial networks. Community can be divided into subgroups including the arts, business, government, leisure, media, and professions. Note the names of people known from each of these groups who might be interested in joining forces. Involving others distributes advocacy tasks and helps build a strong base of support. Even before an advocacy plan is put into place, analyze each involved individual's strengths and skills. A good organizer is a must, as is someone with strong interpersonal skills. Creative individuals can be used to invent catchy slogans, initiate advertising campaigns, paint signs, and develop attractive displays of student work. One or more people who are effective speakers, as well as writers, also are essential. Someone with fund development skills also will play a crucial role if monies are needed to accomplish established goals. One person doesn't have to do it all (Lewis & Karnes, 2005). Remember that numbers count in terms of work accomplished and visibility by local, state, and national educational and governmental groups (Roberts & Inman, 2003). As the group grows, the range and availability of resources also increases.

Create an Action Plan

Once a support group has been established, it is time to develop an action plan for the advocacy effort. Determine what the group wants to achieve and develop one or more goals. Decide on the intended message, identify the audience(s), select strategies, and develop evaluation criteria that includes a timeline. Build a process of continuous public relations into the group's advocacy plan (Karnes & Lewis, 1997; Lewis & Karnes, 2005). Roberts and Inman (2003) explained that "the most effective public relations campaigns are multifaceted" (p. 24). Develop a familiarity with the policies that govern gifted education at both local and state levels and the protocol for changing them, because making use of this knowledge has been shown to increase the likelihood of success (Robinson & Moon, 2003). See Appendix A for a sample action plan.

Develop the Intended Message

Everyone working on the plan needs to understand the goal(s) and be well-versed in the context in which it was made in order to provide clear explanations to the group's targeted people or groups. This message needs to be consistent regardless of who is advocating so there is no chance of sending mixed messages that could confuse the public and diminish the group's efforts (Lewis & Karnes, 2005).

Identify the Audience

Next, identify the audiences inside and outside of the school that can impact the group's goal(s) and target these individuals when delivering the selected advocacy message. Lewis and Karnes (2005) suggested appraising the intended audience's knowledge level and likelihood of support for the goal(s) in order to better formulate the best way the message should be presented. Remember to include those members of the community who may oppose the plan, as it also is beneficial to speak and listen to potential opponents in order to prepare future counterarguments. In essence, being proactive is more effective than being reactive.

Develop Evaluation Criteria

Evaluation criteria need to be agreed upon in order to determine if the selected goals have been achieved. Decide on a reasonable timeline for completion of each component of the plan (Lewis & Karnes, 2005). Select the strategies that will be employed and the criteria for evaluating them. Goals are separate from the strategies utilized, yet the methods that are employed will influence the likelihood of success and will have an impact on how long attaining a specific goal may take.

One of the easiest ways to organize advocacy strategies and thus facilitate evaluation is to use either a weekly or monthly calendar on which the specific strategy, person responsible, evaluation criteria, and beginning and ending dates are indicated. Select a calendar with plenty of room to write or create your own so each component can be listed along with the evaluation method with space available to add changes or recommendations for future use, as well as feedback on the strategy's success.

Check off each strategy as it is completed and evaluate for timeliness and effectiveness. Effectiveness can be measured at two levels, formative and summative. For the purpose of advocacy, formative evaluation can be viewed as the targets' attention and response to the message. Summative evaluation would be a change in the targets' behavior with regard to gifted students and their education. Was the strategy, such as delivery of fact sheets to teachers' mailboxes, accomplished on time? Were many of the papers tossed in the trash or did teachers keep them long enough to read? Were teachers seen reading the fact sheets? If so, what kinds of comments were heard? Was the feedback basically positive or negative? If possible, note who appears on each end of the spectrum. Proponents can be asked if they would like to join the advocacy effort, and opponents can be interviewed to determine the reasons for their disagreement. Either way, useful information can be gained or opposition to the intended message might be lessened.

Finally, when the advocacy plan has been completed, was the goal achieved? This is the summative evaluation. Was there greater understanding for and support of gifted education? Did that support result in the desired change, such as the expansion of the gifted program? (See Figure 1 for a basic evaluation form.)

Select Advocacy Strategies

Lewis and Karnes (2005) discussed a wide array of strategies categorized as using print media, nonprint media, and other media. The choice of a strategy or several strategies should be based on the target audience. Consider which method(s) appear to have the best chance of capturing the attention of the target audience. Another consideration is the believability of sources. Would a newspaper article, a public service announcement on the radio or local TV station, a message sent home with students, or some novel approach be most likely to be an effective dissemination method given the nature of the message and who is being targeted? Remember that just because a method is easy or free does not make it the best selection. Take time to consider the goals, the nature of the message, and the willingness of the

Goal:

Strategies	Start/End Dates	Person Responsible	Criteria	Results

Figure 1. Sample evaluation form.

selected audience when deciding on the most efficient method of distribution.

Print Media

A wealth of print media choices are available in publications by Karnes and Lewis (1997) and Lewis and Karnes (2005). Many of those options, as well as new ones, are briefly described here. What is the intended goal? What needs to be publicized: Student achievements? An organization's meeting schedule? Featured speakers? The selection of specific print media will be guided by the desired public relations or advocacy outcome. Choices for individuals, as well as groups, might include:

- *Articles* on a wide range of topics in newsletters for the school and other organizations at both the local and state level, newspapers, magazines, and journals. A short article about gifted children's typical characteristics and a few instructional recommendations that meet their needs can be offered to another organization's newsletter (e.g., reading teachers, elementary education teachers, school counselors) in exchange for one of that group's articles in the gifted/talented newsletter.
- *Editorials* written for a local newspaper or an organization's newsletter. Check the newspaper's writer's guidelines.
- *E-mails* to individuals or large groups.
- *Fact sheets* are usually pithy, one-page papers on a focused topic that are organized using headings and bullets to make them easy to read. Briefly highlight key facts about cognitive and affective characteristics and their effects on learning and social interactions. Create several early on so they can be used as a basis for other public relations and advocacy efforts. A popular fact sheet is Bright Child vs. Gifted Learner (see http://www.memphis-schools.k12.tn.us/admin/curriculum/clue/comparison.html), and another is a list of common myths and truths about gifted

and talented learners (see http://www.hoagiesgifted.org/eric/fact/myths.html).

- *Faxes* can quickly send a letter to notify legislators and other decision makers about your concerns regarding pending legislation or to thank them for continued support.
- *Letters* to individuals, groups, and to the editor of the local newspaper (see Appendix B for a sample letter to the editor from parents). The Kentucky Association for Gifted Education posts a model letter to the editor on their association Web site (see http://www.wku.edu/kage/whitepaper.html/WhitePaperEditor.pdf).
- *Op-Ed* or a commentary piece is published opposite the editorial page and is used to call attention to current issues and educate the public about them. Such articles may be used to inform others about local, state, or national advocacy issues and may include a call to action if written by an organized group.
- *Posters* advertising a meeting or sharing information about gifted learners.
- *School bulletin board displays* of student work (Besnoy, 2005).
- *Web pages,* both personal and school, or personal space on public, interactive Web sites such as MySpace. School Web pages should include the local definition of giftedness, program descriptions, personal pages of teachers, samples of student work, and links to state and national associations' Web sites. Support materials for parents, students, and other teachers also would be desirable, including reading materials, online activities for students, and suggested summer and academic year enrichment programs.

An advocacy group would have the people power and resources to add to the above list. This group might want to employ one or more of the following:

- *Advertising* can be paid for or underwritten by a willing sponsor and can appear in newspapers, magazines, or on billboards. Such outlets can be used to inform the general public about major issues as part of a large advocacy campaign.
- *Blogs* linked to an organization's Web site provide interactive communication; specific topics may be arranged and the schedule posted and e-mailed to members or Listserv subscribers.
- *Bookmarks* with a logo and a catchy phrase or with a list of characteristics of the gifted are relatively inexpensive and can be given away to large groups from educators, counselors, or business people, to legislators, medical personnel, the media, the library, or other organization members.
- *Brochures or flyers* about a gifted program can detail the benefits of joining a local or state organization or the key characteristics and needs of gifted children and can be circulated in schools, the administration building, in medical or counseling office waiting rooms, and the like.
- *Bumper stickers* can be used to show group membership, provide information about the needs of gifted learners using a catchy slogan, or advocate for or against a piece of legislation or public policy.
- *Bus placards,* both inside and outside, can be used in much the same way as billboards as part of a comprehensive advocacy campaign.
- *Buttons* with a logo or saying can be used to identify group members. More versatile than T-shirts, they can be used for many of the same purposes. They have the advantage of being worn more often and more places than T-shirts and can be used to advocate for or against a particular initiative.
- *Handbooks* describing identification methods, educational strategies, or program components can be made available

in printed, HTML, or PDF format on a school or organization's Web site and will attract and educate readers.

- *News releases* can be circulated to alert the media about upcoming special events, opinion pieces, and human interest stories.
- *Novelty items* such as pencils, pens, Post-it® notes, dry erase boards, magnets, mugs, hats, sun visors, and the like can be printed with a group's name, logo, and a support statement and used as "giveaways" at various events.
- *Piggyback mailings* can be used to include a brochure, fact sheet, bookmark, or other material within other mailings, such as utility bills, to reach a broad audience.
- *Position papers* may be drafted in conjunction with other organizations to document support for gifted education.
- *Postcards* can be used to remind members of meetings or share characteristics or accomplishments of gifted children in text or graphic form through the mail, in teachers' mailboxes, or as centerpieces at conferences.
- *Scrapbooks* can be assembled to document the opportunities and benefits of gifted education in a school. The scrapbook can be displayed at the district office, at PTA/PTO meetings, school open houses, and other school or community events (Bisland, 2003).
- *Social networking Web sites* such as Facebook.com and MySpace.com can be used to discuss views about gifted education and provide broad exposure. This is an underutilized resource gaining popularity among a wide range of individuals.
- *Stickers* with a logo, group name, and appeal to vote for or against a piece of legislation can be placed on envelopes, folders, windows, cars, on oneself, and others.
- *T-shirts* can be used to show group membership for both adults and students, for school support when a team participates in academic competitions, or when appearing

at other organizations such as school board meetings or visiting legislators.

- *Web Quests* (Web-based instructional units) are gaining in popularity. They can be designed by computer-adept teachers or their students as a teaching tool for staff development or for presentations to professional and business groups (see http://webquest.org for background and examples).

- *Web sites* can be used to provide insight regarding gifted students, their needs, and their education; they can be linked to the Web sites of the school district, the state gifted organization, the state department of education, Chamber of Commerce, and community businesses and organizations that recognize the benefits of quality education for gifted learners.

- *White papers* (longer extensions of position papers) are publications that present the philosophy of a group on a specific subject. An important consideration when writing a white paper is to be objective—white papers should include citations of outside sources, contain key details that will inform without overwhelming the reader, and use carefully crafted language that neither assumes extensive prior knowledge nor patronizes the reader (Hoffman Marketing Communications, n.d.). Sample white papers relevant to gifted education can be found at http://www.wku.edu/kage/whitepaper.html/ whitepaper.pdf and http://www.tip.duke.edu/resources/ Tapestry_of_Talent.pdf.

- *Wikipedia* is a free, online encyclopedia that allows anyone to edit entries to increase accuracy and coverage of topics. This resource offers opportunities to reach a wide audience and provides an excellent opportunity to correct misinformation.

- *Wire services* can be used to spread news messages from one community to another, usually disseminating items such as important news stories to a range of newspapers.

Nonprint Media

These are auditory and sometimes graphic media employed to build public awareness that also can be used for advocacy. Lewis and Karnes (2005) and Karnes and Lewis (1997) each described many examples of these useful strategies. Other technology-based strategies include closed circuit television, podcasts, YouTube, and the school intercom.

- *Closed circuit television* is similar to the school intercom; gifted students could use this electronic source to deliver the morning school news, including notices of special events and accomplishments for all school programs, and learn broadcasting skills at the same time.
- *Computer graphics* can be created by students, teachers, parents, or professionals to use for logos on bookmarks, brochures, buttons, T-shirts, Web sites, and other print media.
- *Podcasts*, a newer auditory or auditory with visual supports medium, can be downloaded from a Web site or "pushed" to subscribers as MP3 files and played on any of the popular MP3 players, including some cell phones and Personal Desk Assistants (PDAs). Podcasts can provide short informational segments to entire staff developments and classes.
- *Radio* can be used to broadcast community calendars, feature stories, interviews, news, public service announcements (PSAs), or talk shows. It is a useful outlet because most people listen to the radio sometime during the day and it has the potential of repetitions during the day and week. PSAs are short, 15–20-second announcements of upcoming events that may be aired several times a day. Usually, the text is prerecorded and delivered to the station as a digital audio file.
- *School intercoms* may be used to inform the student body about special events and activities (Besnoy, 2005); gifted students might be responsible for the day's announcements.

- *Telephones* provide person-to-person communication, especially when organized into a calling tree; advocates can rapidly disseminate critical information through phone calls.
- *Telephone answering machines* offer the option of creating a recorded message. The phone number can be advertised at specific times for individuals to call in to listen.
- *Television* uses are similar to radio with the advantage of seeing participants involved in the feature stories, interviews, and news; it does not have the wide range of radio; a calendar of events may be auditory or a text bulletin board of events; dedicated community channels are a good source for adults and students to be interviewed about current projects or to air advocacy issues.
- *Videos* may be developed by students, teachers, parents, or professionals to show classroom activities and special events for later broadcast by the news media or played on closed circuit television as a display at open houses and conferences. If digital, a video may be saved to DVDs to be shared through the mail or converted to QuickTime or Windows Media Player files, saved on a server, and linked to school or district Web sites.
- *Webcams* can capture classroom or special events without the need for a videographer; digital files can be used like other digital video.
- *YouTube,* a public video Web site, makes digital video available to a wide audience. Currently, this new medium is used by the youth culture; however, businesses are beginning to use it as a marketing tool and gifted program supporters can, too.

Other Media

As with print and nonprint media, Lewis and Karnes (2005) and Karnes and Lewis (1997) describe other media that can enhance strategies for both public relations and advocacy.

- *Displays* can range from student work and competition trophies, to a scrapbook and informational materials, both text and video. They may be housed in the classroom, school or district offices, conferences, libraries, and store or business windows.
- *Special events* include

    > booths at conferences or malls, contests, conferences, panel discussions, proclamations (governor announces state gifted month, mayor names local gifted week), ribbon cutting or wrapping, recognition ceremonies for supporters, recognition of student or class contributions to the community, seminars, sponsorships, staff development, workshops. (Lewis & Karnes, 2005, p. 626)

- *Speeches* can be delivered with or without a PowerPoint presentation at the school and for "business, civic, education, [and] social groups" or education conferences for groups ranging from local to international (Lewis & Karnes, 2005, p. 626).
- *Student performances* can be given at a variety of events, from the local PTO/PTA, to national and international service clubs. Activities might include community arts programs, education conferences, fairs, mall events, or meetings of various organizations.
- *VIP tours* can be given by gifted students for invited dignitaries. Bisland (2003) describes training students to be school tour guides that take visitors to different classrooms and describe the key programs that provide powerful learning opportunities for students, including the gifted program.

Many options abound at the local, state, national, and even the international level where one can advocate for gifted students. The local level is a good place to begin. Working within the neighborhood school, becoming involved in or beginning a parent support group, and working within the larger community are three possible venues. The local community can be approached from several perspectives: various organizations regardless of their focus, businesses and industry, and local government. The names of these groups and contact people within them usually are available through the Chamber of Commerce. Members of these groups can be both target audiences and present and future allies.

If a larger reach is desired, consider joining the state gifted association (see http://www.nagc.org/index.aspx?id=609&gbs for a listing of state organizations). State organizations always are looking for members interested in becoming involved in building stronger programs for gifted learners and in advocacy that is needed to foster improvement statewide. Working alone or with like-minded advocates, one can e-mail, write letters, phone, and visit state legislators. By staying current on legislation that affects education in general and any laws specifically dealing with gifted education, members can respond quickly to legislative initiatives. Individuals should focus on the representatives from their respective district by getting to know them, applauding their efforts, and knowledgeably discussing differences of opinion on the issues. If a legislator has been particularly supportive of gifted education, be sure to thank that person—even when the support doesn't apply locally. Such actions help build good relationships for the times when that person's support may be needed.

Another state-level advocacy platform is other education organizations, such as those made up of specific content areas, as well as those for administrators, counselors, and parents. Enhancing the connections with some of the members of these groups and developing new contacts begins to move knowledge and messages of support outside of the gifted education arena. A great deal can be learned about intersecting values and goals through these contacts. Publishing information in one another's group newsletters and serving as guest speakers at the conferences of other organizations can build a collateral of good will among both sets of colleagues (Karnes & Lewis, 1997; Lewis & Karnes, 2005). Riley and Karnes (1993) surveyed organizations within one state to determine their interest in and support for gifted education. Although many were supportive and wanted to learn more about gifted children and their education, no organization at that time had adopted a position statement supporting gifted education. Networking with other associations remains an underutilized resource ripe for exploration.

Many of the state-level strategies also can be used at the national level. Consider joining and becoming active in one of the national support organizations such as the National Association for Gifted Children (NAGC) and the Council for Exceptional Children (CEC). Each organization has several divisions of divergent and specialized interest. The Association for the Gifted (TAG) is the division within CEC whose focus is on gifted education. Both NAGC and CEC have informative Web sites, journals that come with membership, annual conferences, and an international reach. Parents and teachers can find the information they crave, meet like-minded members, and discover numerous opportunities to advocate for gifted children. Keeping Congressional representatives and senators informed about the importance of gifted education and thanking them for their continued support can foster attention at the national, as well as state, level.

No matter which level one becomes involved in while advocating for the needs of gifted children, the opportunities are many and satisfying. A little bit or a lot—everyone can help.

When Can I Advocate?

Now would be a good time to begin planning how to become involved. For one's first foray into advocacy, be it a small supporting part, initiating a major project, or anything in between—just get going and do it!

One act of advocacy can affect a few people. Regular, planned communications can cause positive change. Using the school calendar, coordinate one or two activities for students, teachers, or others with events already scheduled on the school calendar (e.g., open house, a holiday, PTA/PTO meeting). In subsequent years, expand by adding one or two additional activities. When advocates involve themselves in already scheduled activities, their participation becomes more meaningful, and their cumulative efforts will more effectively emphasize to the public the need for appropriate education for gifted learners.

Conclusion

Equal opportunity in education need not mean the same education delivered in the same way at the same time and at the same pace. Educational quality also can mean equal opportunity to learn at a challenge level and in a manner that is developmentally appropriate, a target that differs from one child to the next. Teachers need not teach every child individually in order to reach this goal. It does mean that educators need to take into consideration that all children are not the same and plan differentiated lessons for a range of abilities—lessons that are more open-ended with alternative ways to accomplish learning. Some students will need more structure to scaffold their learning, and others will thrive on less guidance and more open-ended options. To truly serve the needs of *all* students, educators will need to learn more about student differences and how to accommodate those differences.

Gifted children are students whose educational needs have too frequently been ignored. Increasing teachers', school officials', and the general public's awareness of how gifted learners differ educationally and affectively pays big dividends in gaining community respect for gifted programs and their enrollees.

Advocacy is the tool. Become educated about the cognitive and affective characteristics of children who are gifted and the educational options that are available. Become a supporter and advocate for positive change in education so that *all* children learn at a high level, especially children who are gifted.

Web Sites

Advocacy Sites

Gifted Association of Missouri (GAM):
Successful Advocacy
http://www.mogam.org/www/advocacy.shtml

Provides brief instructions on how to advocate, directions on writing a letter to a legislator with a sample, how to call a legislator, and how to hold a meeting.

Gifted Mandates by State or Province
http://www.hoagiesgifted.org/mandates.htm

Contains state and some Canadian gifted and talented information, including mandates for identification, program, level, twice-exceptional service, and early college/dual enrollment.

Hoagies' Gifted Education Page: Advocacy

http://www.hoagiesgifted.org/advocacy.htm

Offers dozens of links to books and articles that assist with advocacy for gifted children. One of many pages providing extensive, well-organized, and searchable links to online resources.

Note the Difference: Bright Child vs. Gifted Learner

http://www.memphis-schools.k12.tn.us/admin/curriculum/clue/comparison.html

Educators and parents need to study this chart that compares bright students (top learners in class) with gifted students. It clearly shows the difference in the way they learn, while not being critical of the students.

Is It a Cheetah?

http://www.stephanietolan.com/is_it_a_cheetah.htm

Gifted specialist, writer, and advocate Stephanie Tolan compares gifted children to cheetahs in a very effective way.

Kentucky Association for Gifted Education

http://www.wku.edu/kage

Links to a white paper, letter to the editor, and other resources.

National Association for Gifted Children (NAGC)

http://www.nagc.org

Excellent resource for parents, teachers, and experts in gifted and talented education including an annual conference, information on summer programs, and multiple publications. Useful advocacy information is found in the sections that follow:

Advocacy Toolkit

http://www.nagc.org/index.aspx?id=36

Contains a link to working with the media, and lists eight areas that need to be considered when planning for advocacy including a thorough legislative update; each section is further explained and some have additional components.

Designing a Gifted Program
http://www.nagc.org/index.aspx?id=2027

Another link to the Pre-K–Grade12 Program Standards that should guide program development and can be used to congratulate programs that meet some or all of these standards and used as a model for what should be in place for gifted learners.

NAGC Positions Statements
http://www.nagc.org/index.aspx?id=375

Lists NAGC's position regarding many areas critical to gifted education, from ability grouping and acceleration, to preservice teacher education programs and using tests to identify gifted students. Each one can serve as a model for developing a group's own position statement or used as fact sheets.

State Association Web Sites
http://www.nagc.org/index.aspx?id=609&gbs

Lists all state associations and provides links to each. Note that some states have more than one state association.

Working With the Media
http://www.nagc.org/index.aspx?id=1004

Describes how to write news stories, commentary (Op-Ed) pieces, and letters to the editor.

Nebraska Association for Gifted (NAG): Successful Advocacy
http://www.negifted.org/4953.html

Describes steps for successful advocacy adapted from the Missouri state organization and posted with their permission. Good example of linking state information to the basic steps. Under "Educate Yourself," this site provides a link briefly describing the history of gifted education in the state. Under "Communicate Your Message," a link takes the reader to NAG's position on gifted education. Various national and state leaders can be found under the "Identify Targets" section.

Texas Association for the Gifted and Talented (TAGT): Effective Advocacy

http://www.txgifted.org/displaycommon.cfm?an=1&subarticlenbr=35

Provides three very useful links to PDF files with informative annotations: "A Checklist for Advocating with Public Policy Makers," "Supporting Gifted Education Through Advocacy," and "Advocating for Appropriate Education for Your Child." Also includes links to the "Code & Regulation" for gifted education in Texas. Under "Legislation," the organization's position on legislative policy and advice for advocates can be found, as well as a link directing advocates on how to "Contact Your Legislator."

Congressional and State Contacts

Congress.org

http://www.congress.org

Type in your zip code for links to the President, congressional representatives and senators, state governors, and state representatives. Party affiliation and relevant districts are noted. Click on any of the links for the individual's Web page that includes e-mail using a Web form. A "Take Action by Issue" selection is provided and many other useful links.

Contacting the Congress

http://www.visi.com/juan/congress

Another way to gain access to state members of Congress. Click on the state for phone, fax, and Web pages (lists all Representatives);

or type in street address, city, and zip code and select state for senators and specific representative.

State Legislatures Internet Links
http://www.ncsl.org/public/leglinks.cfm

Select state and desired content area (nine areas in addition to the home page) to access links to information from state legislatures.

Gifted Centers and Institutes

Belin–Blank International Center for Gifted Education and Talent Development at the University of Iowa
http://www.education.uiowa.edu/belinblank

Includes information about this center at the University of Iowa, links for students, educators, parents, calendar of events, and breaking news. Offers talent search and summer programs, and links to update on the impact of *A Nation Deceived*.

**Center for Gifted Education
at the College of William and Mary**
http://www.cfge.wm.edu

Provides information about the center, curriculum developed by the center, ongoing research, and links for educators (including professional development) and gifted students.

**Center for Gifted Studies
at Western Kentucky University**
http://www.wku.edu/Dept/Support/AcadAffairs/Gifted/cmsmadesimple

Information about the center and links for students (Saturday, summer, and travel study programs), parents (resources, travel study program, legislative alert), teachers (trainings, Advanced Placement Institute), and alumni.

Davidson Institute
http://www.ditd.org

Located in Reno, NV, this institute was developed to help highly gifted learners. "Getting Started for Parents," summer programs, scholarship program, young scholars' program for profoundly gifted students, online publications, and *Genius Denied* (book published by the Davidsons about the frustrations of being gifted and wasting time in school "learning" what they already know) are all accessible.

Twelve Cost Effective Educational Options for Serving Gifted Students
http://www.gt-cybersource.org/Record.aspx?NavID=2_0&rid=14057

Good ideas for advocates and schools stressing several acceleration options, specialized classes that allow for fast-paced, challenging instruction; counseling; Talent Searches; and other academic summer programs.

Centre for Gifted Education at University of Calgary
http://www.ucalgary.ca/~gifted

Provides academic programs for teachers, lecture programs for parents, summer camp programs for students, professional development for schools, information services (resource lists for teachers of elementary and secondary students by content area, articles, reading list for parents, and other resources), access to past and current newsletters, listing of conferences, and a collaborative talent search.

The Frances A. Karnes Center for Gifted Studies at the University of Southern Mississippi
http://www.usm.edu/gifted

Links to services for youth (Saturday and summer programs), parents (conference specifically for parents), and teachers (Day of Sharing, scholarships). Strong emphasis on leadership with summer programs for students and leadership competition, leadership resources and research. Multiple publications sorted by special interests for teachers, parents, and students. Links to low-incidence gifted supports (e.g., overview of gifted/disabled youth with sections on types of disabilities, nonverbal assessment of culturally different gifted, preschool fact sheet).

Gifted Development Center
http://www.gifteddevelopment.com

The Gifted Development Center is headed by Dr. Linda Silverman, a testing expert and researcher. Includes information on giftedness, assessment, visual-spatial learners, books and tapes on aspects of giftedness, and school choices.

Gifted Resource Center of New England
http://www.grcne.com

Good list of links organized for parents and children and teens, as well as educational links; listing of publications on highly gifted learners and ordering instructions.

The Hollingworth Center for Highly Gifted Children
http://www.hollingworth.org

Site is no longer updated; however, the following resources are useful for their special focus on highly gifted children: identification and assessment, bibliographies, special topics, and links to other resources.

National Research Center on the Gifted and Talented (NRC/GT)
http://www.gifted.uconn.edu/nrcgt.html

Past newsletters, articles, brochures, and summaries of numerous important studies (e.g., ability grouping, cooperative learning, best practices for identification and service) are among the many resources.

Neag School of Education, University of Connecticut
http://www.gifted.uconn.edu

Contains links to the National Research Center on the Gifted and Talented; Confratute (a highly respected teacher training program); extensive materials on Dr. Joseph Renzulli's Schoolwide Enrichment Model and Learning System; articles, resources for parents, and considerably more.

University of Louisiana at Lafayette's Center for Gifted Education
http://www.coe.louisiana.edu/centers/gifted.html

Offers academic enrichment mini-courses for students in preschool through eighth grade. One different option is interdisciplinary enrichment classes for Pre-K children lasting 1.5 to 2 hours for 2 weeks. Another is a one-week residential program for seventh and eighth graders to develop academic, creative, and/or leadership skills. Early admission to college is available for 11th-grade students. Workshops for teachers are also provided.

Gifted Organizations

American Association for Gifted Children (AAGC)
http://www.aagc.org

Mission is to provide research-based information on curriculum, programs, and resources for parents and others who support gifted children. Useful for its various articles.

Council for Exceptional Children (CEC)
http://www.cec.sped.org

Primary site for resources for exceptional children, including gifted. Specialized divisions include The Association for Gifted (TAG), parallel site to NAGC. Links to current legislative issues, ERIC Digests focusing on gifted and other exceptionalities, and many other resources.

Gifted Canada

http://www3.bc.sympatico.ca/giftedcanada

Bilingual site (English/French) with links to gifted organizations in the Canadian provinces; teaching links focus on Canada and the United Kingdom, with a "World Sites" section and online manuals offering resources not found elsewhere; Canadian resources, and Canadian researchers and links to their work.

National Association for Gifted Children (NAGC)

http://www.nagc.org

"Get Involved at NAGC" offers opportunities to join the advocacy efforts. Extensive supports for educators and parents, including information and resources, publications, strong advocacy and legislation section, link to state associations and conferences, large national conference with international attendance, list of summer programs.

Supporting Emotional Needs of the Gifted (SENG)

http://www.sengifted.org

"Getting Involved" offers many opportunities to volunteer and learn. Offers articles and other resources for parents and professionals, parent support groups, courses for continuing education, and national conference with social/emotional focus.

Uniquely Gifted

http://uniquelygifted.org

Site is based on book of the same name by Kiesa Kay; provides extensive resources for and about gifted children who are twice- or multiply exceptional.

World Council for Gifted and Talented Children

http://www.worldgifted.ca

Supports a conference and various publications. Useful for its international perspective.

Legal Supports

Family Educational Rights and Privacy Act (FERPA)
http://www.ed.gov/policy/gen/guid/fpco/ferpa/index.html

Explains parents' rights regarding their children's educational records; students have these rights when they become 18 years old. Important information for student and self-advocacy.

Know Your Legal Rights in Gifted Education (ERIC Digest #E541)
http://www.hoagiesgifted.org/eric/e541.html

Gives basic information parents need regarding limited legal support for gifted education; explains negotiation, mediation, due process, and court cases and how to use them.

National Reports

A Nation Deceived: How Schools Hold Back America's Brightest Students (2004, September)
http://www.nationdeceived.org

Analyzes the value of acceleration; provides research support for acceleration as a practice strategy for servicing gifted students. Executive summary is online, each volume is available as a PDF file, and print copies can be requested.

A Nation at Risk: The Imperative for Educational Reform (1983, April)
http://www.ed.gov/pubs/NatAtRisk

Report details need for educational reform. The findings and recommendations sections provide useful information for advocacy.

National Excellence: A Case for Developing America's Talent (1993, October)
http://www.ed.gov/pubs/DevTalent/toc.html

Describes the crisis in U.S. education that still existed 10 years after *A Nation at Risk* was published. Begin with the Executive

Summary, and then read the full report to gain context for advocacy.

Prisoners of Time: Report of the National Education Commission on Time and Learning (1994, April)
http://www.ed.gov/pubs/PrisonersOfTime

This advocacy document describes how U.S. education is controlled by the clock; lists goals, describes lessons learned from other educational systems, offers recommendations, and suggests a better way.

Talent Searches

Most of the talent searches use the ACT EXPLORE test designed for eighth graders as an above-grade-level test for elementary students and the ACT and SAT college entrance exams for seventh–ninth graders. These out-of-level tests give a better picture of gifted students' strengths. There are four regional searches and several independent searches.

Belin–Blank Exceptional Student Talent Search (BESTS)
http://www.education.uiowa.edu/belinblank/talent-search

Above-grade-level testing using the EXPLORE (grades 4–6) and the ACT and SAT (grades 7–9). Provides summer programs for eligible students on the University of Iowa campus. Describes purpose and benefits. Range of classes is available for different age children.

Carnegie Mellon Institute for Talented Elementary and Secondary Students (C-MITES)
http://www.cmu.edu/cmites

Above-grade-level testing for the Elementary Student Talent Search uses the EXPLORE test. Describes criteria for participation and benefits. Summer and weekend classes are available at different sites.

Johns Hopkins University Center for Talented Youth (CTY)

http://cty.jhu.edu/ts

Above-grade-level testing using the School and College Ability Test (SCAT; grades 2–6) and ACT and SAT (grades 7–8). Service areas: AK, AZ, CA, CT, DC, DE, HI, MA, MD, ME, NH, NJ, NY, OR, PA, RI, VA, VT, WA, WV, and international searches. Summer programs and distance education are offered nationally and internationally, family academic conferences are offered for specific grade levels, and other benefits are discussed.

Duke University Talent Identification Program (Duke TIP)

http://www.tip.duke.edu

Above-grade-level testing using the EXPLORE (grades 4–5) and ACT and SAT (grade 7). Service areas: AL, AR, FL, GA, IA, KS, KY, LA, MO, MS, NC, NE, OK, SC, TN, TX, and information for international searches. Offers educational options and many resources including an online newsletter for parents and teachers, *Duke Gifted Letter.*

Rocky Mountain Academic Talent Search (RMTS) at University of Denver's Center for Innovative and Talented Youth

http://www.du.edu/city/programs/academic-year-programs/rocky-mountain-talent-search.html

Above-grade-level testing using the EXPLORE (grades 3–6), ACT, and SAT (grades 6–9). Service areas: CO, ID, MT, NM, NV, UT, WY. Describes procedure and benefits. Process begins in September of each year.

Midwest Academic Talent Search (MATS) at Northwestern University's Center for Talent Development (CTD)
http://www.ctd.northwestern.edu/mats

Above-grade-level testing for students in grades 3–9 using the EXPLORE (grades 3–6) and ACT and SAT (grades 6–9). Service areas: IL, IN, MI, MN, ND, OH, SD, WI. Benefits include information on special educational options. Process begins in early September of each year. Research and resource articles available.

Recommended Reading

Books

Colangelo, N., Assouline, S. G., & Gross, M. U. M. (2004). *A nation deceived: How schools hold back America's brightest students* (Vol. 1). Iowa City, IA: The Connie Belin & Jacqueline N. Blank International Center for Gifted Education and Talent Development. Retrieved April 12, 2007, from http://www.nationdeceived.org

Describes the research base for effectiveness of acceleration for serving gifted children and refutes pervasive beliefs that it is harmful to children.

Davidson, J., Davidson, R., & Vanderkam, L. (2004). *Genius denied: How to stop wasting our brightest young minds.* New York: Simon & Schuster.

Details how the educational system that purports to "leave no child behind" continues to leave gifted and especially highly gifted students with limited appropriate learning opportunities.

Karnes, F. A., & Marquardt, M. G. (1999). *Gifted children and legal issues: An update.* Scottsdale, AZ: Gifted Psychology Press.

Describes mediation, due process, and alternatives to litigation related to gifted and talented education and such specifics as homeschooling problems, Advanced Placement classes, and civil rights.

Kay, K. (2000). *Uniquely gifted: Identifying and meeting the needs of the twice exceptional student.* Gilsum, NH: Avocus.

Guide for understanding and meeting the needs of gifted students who also have needs such as ADHD, Asperger's syndrome, bipolar disorder, learning disabilities, and vision problems.

Kerr, B. (1997). *Smart girls: A new psychology of girls, women, and giftedness.* Scottsdale, AZ: Gifted Psychology Press.

Explains why gifted girls may not work to their potential in adolescence and adulthood. Research is summarized and practical advice for parents is provided to help counter some of the challenges resulting from current society. Includes short biographies of bright women.

Kerr, B., & Cohn, S. J. (2001). *Smart boys: Talent, manhood, and the search for meaning.* Scottsdale, AZ: Great Potential Press.

Describes research and uses interviews with bright men to help explain why smart boys encounter challenges that may cause them to underachieve as adolescents and adults. Realistic advice for parents is included.

Rogers, K. B. (2002). *Re-forming gifted education: How parents and teachers can match the program to the child.* Scottsdale, AZ: Great Potential Press.

Easy-to-read resource written especially for parents and teachers describing how to build more meaning into the gifted child's academic program to help gifted students be successful in K–12 schools that often are ill-prepared to teach them. Chapters cover basic educational information; descriptions of different "kinds" of gifted learners; and more specific guidance on acceleration, grouping, types of programming, out-of-school learning, development of an educational plan, a range of supplementary resources, and more.

Smutny, J. F. (1997). *Teaching young gifted children in the regular classroom: Identifying, nurturing, and challenging ages 4–9.* Minneapolis, MN: Free Spirit.

Includes characteristics of preschool-primary gifted students and instructional strategies for this age group that can be used in a regular classroom.

Tomlinson, C. A. (1999). *The differentiated classroom: Responding to the needs of all learners.* Alexandria, VA: Association for Supervision and Curriculum Development.

Details what differentiation is, why it is needed, and clearly describes multiple strategies for accomplishing high-level instruction for kids with different readiness levels.

Walker, S. Y. (2002). *The survival guide for parents of gifted kids: How to understand, live with, and stick up for your gifted child* (Rev. ed.). Minneapolis, MN: Free Spirit.

Provides clear explanations about the characteristics of giftedness, identification procedures, how to advocate for appropriate education, and advice on parenting.

Webb, J. T., Meckstroth, E., & Tolan, S. S. (1998). *Guiding the gifted child: A practical source for parents and teachers.* Scottsdale, AZ: Gifted Psychology Press.

Parents' guide for raising a gifted child from preschool through adolescence detailing specific advice about relationships with siblings and peers, daily life, discipline, motivation, working with teachers, and children's risk factors such as stress and depression.

Winebrenner, S. (2001). *Teaching gifted kids in the regular classroom: Strategies and techniques every teacher can use to meet the academic needs of the gifted and talented* (Rev. ed.). Minneapolis, MN: Free Spirit.

Practical guide with clear explanations to basic instructional strategies such as curriculum compacting with variations including how to adapt this strategy for different content areas, using contracts and models, hardest first, and much more. Has reproducible masters.

Journal Articles, ERIC Documents, Guides

Davidson Institute for Talent Development. (n.d.). *Advocating for exceptionally gifted young people: A guidebook.* Retrieved May 17, 2007, from http://print.ditd.org/Guidebook1.pdf

The first section describes the expected outcomes of the guide. Section two offers an orientation to advocacy. Other sections focus on chapters from *Re-Forming Gifted Education* by Karen Rogers (see Recommended Books). Sections 6–8 focus specifically on advocacy issues.

Archambault, F. X., Jr., Westberg, K. L., Brown, S. W., Hallmark, B. W., Emmons, C. L., & Zhang, W. (1993). *Regular classroom practices with gifted students: Results of a national survey of classroom teachers* (Research Monograph 93102). Storrs: National Research Center on the Gifted and Talented, University of Connecticut. Retrieved April 12, 2007, from http://www.gifted.uconn.edu/nrcgt/archwest.html

Summarizes the results of a major study; posits that few modifications are made for gifted learners regardless of public or private school; rural, urban, or suburban; geographic location; or concentration of major minority groups.

Karnes, F. A., & Marquardt, R. (1997). *Know your legal rights in gifted education* (ERIC EC Digest #E541). Reston, VA: Council for Exceptional Children. Retrieved May 15, 2007, from http://www.ericdigests.org/1998-2/legal.htm

Provides background on differences between gifted and special education legal protections and describes use of negotiation, mediation, due process, and court cases.

Kulik, J. A. (1992). *An analysis of the research on ability grouping: Historical and contemporary perspectives* (Research–Based Decision Making Series No. 9204). Storrs: National Research Center on the Gifted and Talented, University of Connecticut. Retrieved May 7, 2007, from http://www.gifted.uconn.edu/nrcgt/kulik.html

Details analysis of research on different kinds of ability grouping and provides guidelines for use.

Landrum, M., Callahan, C., & Shaklee, B. (Eds.). (1998). *NAGC pre-K–grade 12 gifted program standards*. Retrieved May 6, 2007, from http://www.nagc.org/index.aspx?id=1863

Describes the standards and how to use them, and provides links to details of the seven individual standards.

Lovecky, D. V. (1994). Exceptionally gifted children: Different minds. *Roeper Review, 17,* 116–120. Retrieved May 17, 2007, from http://www.gifteddevelopment.com/PDF_files/exceptgt.pdf

Details how differently gifted children with very high scores on intelligence tests think and ways some of these characteristics can create problems for these children in school.

Lynch, S. J. (1996). *Should gifted students be grade-advanced?* (ERIC EC Digest #E526). Reston, VA: Council for Exceptional Children. Retrieved May 15, 2007, from http://www.ericdigests.org/1995-1/grade.htm

Provides useful, basic advice on advantages of grade and subject acceleration and when it might not be appropriate. Answers parents' questions about effects on academics, socialization, and teachers' views.

Reis, S. M., Westberg, K. L., Kulikowich, J., Caillard, F., Hébert, T., Plucker, J., et al. (1993). *Why not let high ability students start school in January? The curriculum compacting study* (Research Monograph 93106). Storrs: National Research Center on the Gifted and Talented, University of Connecticut. Retrieved May 15, 2007, from http://www.gifted.uconn.edu/nrcgt/reiswest.html

Summary of research investigating the amount of regular curriculum content that could be eliminated without detriment to gifted learners. Conclusion 3 states, "Approximately 40–50% of traditional classroom material could be eliminated for targeted students in one or more" of the four basic content areas.

Robinson, A. (1991). *Cooperative learning and the academically talented students* (Research-Based Decision Making Series No. 9106). Storrs: National Research Center on the Gifted and Talented, University of Connecticut. Retrieved May, 15, 2007, from http://www.gifted.uconn.edu/nrcgt/robinsoa.html

Short summary of research on cooperative learning with clearly stated recommendations for use with gifted students.

Roedell, W. C. (1990). *Nurturing giftedness in young children* (ERIC EC Digest #E487). Reston, VA: Council for Exceptional Children. Retrieved May 15, 2007, from http://www.ericdigests.org/pre-9216/young.htm

Specific descriptions of behaviors of gifted preschoolers and why they occur. Explains uneven development of cognitive, affective, and physical aspects of gifted children in relation to their chronological ages.

Silverman, L. K. (1992). *How parents can support gifted children* (ERIC EC Digest #E515). Reston, VA: Council for Exceptional Children. Retrieved May 15, 2007, from http://www.ericdigests.org/1993/parents.htm

Defines giftedness as asynchronous development and what this means, lists characteristics and explains parental response to them, describes relationships, school placement, and parent advocacy.

Webb, J. T. (1994). *Nurturing social emotional development of gifted children* (ERIC EC Digest #E527). Reston, VA: Council for Exceptional Children. Retrieved May 15, 2007, from http://www.ericdigests.org/1995-1/social.htm

Describes giftedness from the perspective of family, school, and culture, noting strengths that also can create problems, what they are, and how parents can work to prevent them.

Westburg, K. L., & Daoust, M. E. (2003, Fall). The results of the replication of the Classroom Practices Survey replication in two states. *The National Research Center on the Gifted and Talented Newsletter.* Retrieved May 19, 2007, from http://www.gifted.uconn.edu/nrcgt/newsletter/fall03/fall032.html

Disturbing results show teachers still don't teach gifted learners any differently than they do average ability students, even though the teachers in this study had more training than in the original study. Also, responses show that many teachers believe a small amount of time in a special program, even if infrequent, is sufficient to meet the needs of gifted learners.

Winebrenner, S., & Devlin, B. (2001). *Cluster grouping of gifted students: How to provide full-time services on a part-time budget: Update 2001* (ERIC Digest #E607). Reston, VA: Council for Exceptional Children. Retrieved May 15, 2007, from http://www.hoagiesgifted.org/eric/e607.html

Details how to use cluster grouping of several gifted children in a regular classroom.

Besnoy, K. (2005). Using public relations strategies to advocate for gifted programming in your school. *Gifted Child Today, 28*(1), 32–37.

Bisland, A. (2003). Student-created public relations for gifted education. *Gifted Child Today, 26*(2), 60–64.

Clark, B. (2008). *Growing up gifted: Developing the potential of children at home and at school* (7th ed.). Upper Saddle, NJ: Pearson.

Gallagher, J. J. (1997). Least restrictive climate and gifted students. *Peabody Journal of Education, 72*(3/4), 153–165.

Gallagher, J. J., & Gallagher, S. A. (1994). *Teaching the gifted child*. Boston: Allyn & Bacon.

Gross, M. U. M. (2002). "Play partner" or "sure shelter": What gifted children look for in friendship. *The SENG Newsletter, 2*(2) 1–3.

Hoagies' Gifted Education Page. (n.d.). *Gifted education mandates, by state or province.* Retrieved May 22, 2007, from http://www.hoagiesgifted.org/mandates.htm

Hoffman Marketing Communications. (n.d.). *How to write a white paper: A closer look at white paper definition.* Retrieved May 11, 2007, from http://www.hoffmanmarcom.com/closerlook.php

Karnes, F. A., & Lewis, J. (1995). Examining the media coverage of gifted education. *Gifted Child Today, 18*(6), 28–30, 40.

Karnes, F. A., & Lewis, J. D. (1996). Staff development through videotapes in gifted education. *Roeper Review, 19,* 106–110.

Karnes, F. A., & Lewis, J. D. (1997, May). *Public relations: A necessary tool for advocacy in gifted education* (ERIC Digest E542). Retrieved March 25, 2007, from http://www.hoagiesgifted.org/eric/e542.html

Karnes, F. A., Lewis, J. D., & Stephens, K. R. (1999). Parents and teachers working together for advocacy through public relations. *Gifted Child Today, 22*(1), 14–18.

Karnes, F. A., & Stephens, K. R. (2000). *The ultimate guide for student product development & evaluation.* Waco, TX: Prufrock Press.

Kiger, L. (1998). Public relations for gifted education. *Gifted Child Today, 21*(5), 42–44.

Kowalski, T. J. (1996). *Public relations in educational organizations.* Englewood Cliffs, CA: Merrill.

Lewis, J. D., Cruzeiro, P. A., & Hall, C. A. (2007). Impact of two elementary principals' leadership on gifted education in their buildings. *Gifted Child Today, 30*(2), 56–62.

Lewis, J. D., & Karnes, F. A. (1996). *A portrayal of the gifted in magazines: An initial analysis.* (ERIC Document Reproduction Service No. ED405710)

Lewis, J. D., & Karnes, F. A. (2005). Public relations and advocacy for the gifted. In S. M. Bean & F. A. Karnes (Eds.), *Methods and materials for teaching the gifted* (2nd ed., pp. 615–656). Waco, TX: Prufrock Press.

Meadows, S., & Karnes, F. A. (1992). Influencing public opinion of gifted education through the newspaper. *Gifted Child Today, 15*(1), 44–45.

National Association for Gifted Children. (n.d.). *10 common gifted education myths.* Retrieved May 15, 2007, from http://www.nagc.org/index.aspx?id=569

O'Connell-Ross, P. (1993). *National excellence: A case for developing America's talent.* Washington, DC: U.S. Department of Education, Office of Educational Research and Improvement.

Riley, T. L., & Karnes, F. A. (1993). Joining together with other associations: Strategies for cooperation. *Roeper Review, 15,* 250–251.

Roberts, J., & Inman, T. (2003, March). Building advocacy with a public relations campaign. *Parenting for High Potential,* 24–27.

Robinson, A., & Moon, S. M. (2003). National study of local and state advocacy in gifted education. *Gifted Child Quarterly, 47,* 8–25.

Roeper, A. (1986). The administrator in the school for the gifted. *Roeper Review, 9,* 4–10.

Silverman, L. K. (1993). *Counseling the gifted & talented.* Denver, CO: Love.

Troxclair, D., & Karnes, F. A. (1997). Public relations: Advocating for gifted students. *Gifted Child Today, 20*(3), 38–41, 50.

Immediate Goal: To extend the elementary gifted and talented program through the middle school grades.

Ultimate Goal: To develop a comprehensive gifted and talented program for preschool through 12th grade.

Message: Gifted children are gifted all the time; therefore, they need instruction targeted to their instructional level most of the time—the same as all children. Continuous challenge throughout school equals prepared citizens.

Audiences: Focus will be on the immediate goal with some advocacy directed to the pre-Kindergarten and high school groups to build awareness for the next advocacy phase.
- educators (with selected materials targeted to middle school): building principals, school counselors, teachers;
- district administrators and school board members;
- parents of current gifted and talented students; and
- general public with emphasis on the Chamber of Commerce so it can advertise quality of school programs

to newcomers, potential new business/industry, and prospective professionals.

Strategies: Because this plan aims to enlarge the gifted program, a needs assessment of parent, educator, administration, and school board member opinions should be conducted. Include an evaluation of the current program, physical and other resources, and extent of the gifted learner's achievement with and without gifted programming based on disaggregated district achievement data. Once those materials have been evaluated, the current plan can be implemented. Note the timeline and person(s) responsible for following each strategy.

- Fact sheets: Develop a fact sheet detailing student characteristics and resulting educational needs; also use the Bright Child vs. Gifted Learner (http://www.memphis-schools.k12.tn.us/admin/curriculum/clue/comparison. html) and Common Myths and Truths About Gifted Students (http://www.hoagiesgifted.org/eric/fact/myths. html) fact sheets. These will be sent to educators, district administrators, school board members, and parents of gifted learners (one every 3 weeks). A fact sheet describing the program options, intended expansion, current Advanced Placement and honors classes, and benefits for preparing students to be competitive for college can be sent to the Chamber of Commerce. [Nance Cunningham; begin September 1, complete December 1.]
- Interviews: Arrange for a gifted spokesperson to be interviewed on the local community television and radio station. Students will practice being interviewed as a class activity and the most effective speakers can be included in the above interviews or arrange an informal interview of the students as a follow-up on the community television channel. [Josh Steiner; begin September 30, complete by October 30.] Hold informal interviews with school principals (begin with elementary and work through high school), middle school counselors, superintendent, assis-

tant superintendent, curriculum specialist, and school board members. Purpose is informational for advocacy committee and for interviewees. [Two to three members will participate, Nance Cunningham will organize; begin September 1, complete by March 1.]

- Editorial: Discuss writing an editorial for the local newspaper and either prepare it according to the newspaper's specifications or work with one of the editors to develop a strong statement of need for the students and benefits for the community. [Koichi Sato; complete by January 30.]
- Articles (news article, feature article): Write an article for the newspaper describing the interviews. May be prepared by an advocacy member or a community news reporter. [Koichi Sato; complete by November 15.] Arrange with the education editor to publish a half or full-page article focusing on the current program, its benefits, and need to for continuation into middle school. [Sarah Sorjham; begin November 1, complete by March 30.]
- Letters (to the editor, to school personnel): Encourage parents to write letters to the editor and to school personnel (principals, administration, school board) describing the benefits of gifted education for their children. [Carlotta Garcia; begin September 15, complete by April 30.] Gifted teachers will instruct their fifth-grade students on writing letters to the editor and school board to advocate for a continuation of programming when they move into the middle school. [Hailey Walker; begin lessons by October 15, complete letter writing by April 1.]
- School Web page: Ask gifted students and adults with the technical skills to update the Web page with an overview of the goal, message, best practices research that supports extending the program into the middle school, benefits for the students, and the community. Include digital pictures of student accomplishments where possible. [Jane and Michael Smith; complete by October 30.]

Evaluation: Each component of the plan needs to be evaluated to confirm implementation and to gather data about its effectiveness in addition to the immediate goal.

Appendix B
Sample Letter to the Editor

Dear Editor:

As concerned parents, we are pleased the XYZ Unified School District has offered a strong elementary education for our two children. Soon our oldest daughter will be moving up to Starr Middle School. Although we have heard many positive things about the quality of education at this school, one area concerns us. There is no gifted program beyond fifth grade. Our children need this stimulation because they both already have mastered the large majority of the curriculum for their respective grades based on the state standards in each subject. Without more challenging instruction, they are only repeating what they already know—and that is not learning.

The elementary-level gifted program has helped maintain our children's interest in learning with challenging instructional opportunities that allow them to explore every unit in greater depth than is possible in the general curriculum. Each year of school affords students greater access to the world of knowledge and middle school is no exception; quite the contrary, opportunities expand. Because learners who are gifted can process new information faster and can make interdisciplinary connections more readily than typical children, they require a more challenging curriculum so they don't waste precious educational time. We hope that the XYZ Unified School District will investigate the needs of gifted learners and respond by extending the gifted program into the middle school and beyond.

All students need to be continually challenged throughout school, including gifted learners.

Sincerely,
Bob and Carol Jones
4 Tradewinds Drive
XYZ City, State

Joan D. Lewis is associate professor of teacher education at the University of Nebraska at Kearney where she directs the graduate program in gifted education for the University of Nebraska system. She has published articles on a variety of topics and speaks frequently at local, state, national, and international conferences in the areas of alternative assessment, gifted girls, public relations and advocacy, and uses of technology in education. Dr. Lewis' most recent research focuses on the impact school principals have on gifted education. Her work with local and state associations in gifted education has spanned more than 25 years.

Printed in the United States
by Baker & Taylor Publisher Services